Rachel Carson

Who Loved the Sea

by Jean Lee Latham

illustrated by Victor Mays

GARRARD PUBLISHING COMPANY
CHAMPAIGN, ILLINOIS

The Discovery Books are prepared
under the educational supervision of

Mary C. Austin, Ed.D.
Professor of Education
University of Hawaii
Honolulu

Rachel Carson: Who Loved the Sea

Contents

Chapter 1

"Tagalong"

A gentle hand shook Rachel. Mama whispered, "Rachel, dear."

Rachel opened her eyes. It was dark. "What's wrong?"

"Nothing, dear. You said you wanted to hear the birds wake up. You said today was special."

"Oh, yes!"

Soon mama led the way into the dark woods with a flashlight. They sat on their favorite log. Mama switched off the light.

"When will they wake up?" Rachel whispered.

"Any minute now."

Rachel heard a sleepy little twitter, then another one. "Hello, birds!" she called softly. "And good-bye! I can't play here all day anymore. I'm six! I'm going to school! In two days!"

Now all the birds were singing.

"It's just like they were talking back to me! How many birds do we have?"

"Goodness knows," mama said. "We have over 50 acres of woodland. There must be thousands of birds."

"And all of them talking back to me!"

"Yes, dear."

After a while they went back to the kitchen. There was a big calendar on the wall. It said SEPTEMBER 1913.

6

Mama had put a red ring around the number 8, and a black X through the numbers 1, 2, 3, 4, and 5. Now she put an X through 6.

"Only two more days," Rachel said. "Then I'll go to school!"

After breakfast her big brother Robert said, "You want to go to the store with me?"

"Oh, yes!"

Papa said, "Remember, Robert . . ."

Robert grinned. "I know. It's more than half a mile to Springdale. My legs are long. I must not walk too fast."

As they went down the hill, Rachel skipped along ahead of Robert, singing softly, "Only two more days!"

But when they started home from the store, Rachel was very quiet.

What had the ladies meant? She

knew they had been talking about her.

"What's got your lip out?" Robert asked.

"Nothing." She began to sing again and tried to forget the ladies.

That afternoon mama made ginger cookies. Rachel sat on a high stool by the kitchen table. What had the ladies meant?

Mama took a pan of cookies out of the oven. "As soon as they're cool, you may have one."

"I'm not hungry."

Mama dusted off her hands and felt Rachel's forehead. "No, no fever. What's wrong, dear?"

"I'm not hungry."

Mama just waited.

"Mama, what is a 'poor little tagalong'?"

8

"My goodness, where did you hear that?"

"Down at the store. One lady said, 'Carson's poor little tagalong.' Is it something bad?"

"Oh, no, no! It just means that you are lots younger than the other children. Marian is sixteen, and Robert is fourteen."

"It's all right to be a tagalong?"

"Of course."

"And another lady said, 'She won't be so lonesome now.' What's lonesome?"

"That means you're sad when you're alone. They were thinking that you are alone a lot because our land is out from town."

"But I'm not sad! I have all the woods and the birds and the rabbits and—and everything. I'm not lonesome."

"I know. I think you are a lucky

little girl. You have all this lovely woods, only eighteen miles from Pittsburgh!"

"Yes! I *am* lucky!" She ate a cookie. She looked at the calendar. "Only two more days and I go to school. In three days I can read!"

Mama chuckled. "Not quite that soon, dear."

"How many days?"

"Some children learn to read in a few months. Some learn in about a year."

A year? A whole year? Maybe not till she was seven? That would be awful!

Chapter 2

Rachel Makes Up
Her Mind

Long before Rachel was seven, she had read a lot of books. By the time she was eight, she could read some things in Robert's magazine, *St. Nicholas*. The part she liked best was The St. Nicholas League. It gave the names of all the girls and boys who had sent stories to *St. Nicholas*. The best stories were printed in the magazine. And the name of the author was there, and the age: John Jones, age eleven. Mary Smith, age twelve.

How long till she would be eleven? She counted up. Three whole years.

By the time she was nine, she could read things in papa's newspaper. But she didn't like it much. In 1916 a big war was going on in Europe.

Rachel was glad the war was clear across the ocean. She had never seen the ocean, but she knew about it. It was big! Bigger than anything else in the whole world!

"I'm glad the war is clear across the ocean," she said one night. "It won't come over here, will it?"

Papa sighed. "We hope not."

Marian said, "But papa, President Wilson is keeping us out of the war!"

"He's doing his best to keep us out." Papa got up. "Come on. Let's sing."

Mama smiled and went to the piano. Sometimes Rachel sang with them.

Sometimes she shut her eyes and listened. Everybody said they had beautiful voices.

For a while they sang together. Then mama began to play one of Rachel's favorite songs: "Rocked in the Cradle of the Deep." Papa always sang it alone in his deep, rumbly voice.

When the song ended, Rachel gave a big sigh. Songs and poems about the sea were the best of all. Someday she would see the ocean!

Mama said, "Bedtime, dear."

"Just a little while? Just half an hour?"

Marian laughed. "I know what she wants." She brought a book of poems by John Masefield.

Mama read the poems that Rachel loved the best.

Then Rachel got up without a word,

kissed them all good night, and tiptoed upstairs. If she didn't jar her head, she might dream about the ocean.

By the spring of 1917, Rachel didn't want to dream about the ocean. America was in the war. Submarines sneaked through the ocean and blew up ships.

She missed Robert. He was in the army, learning to be a flier. Every week he wrote a long letter home. How they all gathered around mama to hear her read it!

One letter told about a brave English flier. He had been in fierce battles. Now he was in America, training our fliers.

"I'll bet he's glad he can help win the war without getting shot at anymore!" Robert wrote.

The next day another letter came from Robert—a very thin one. The brave young English flier had been killed in an accident.

Rachel went up to her room. She got out her tablet and pencil. She started to write, stopped, crossed out the words, and started again. It was hard to make a story say what you felt! Three times she started over again.

At last the story was done. She made a fresh copy. She showed it to mama. "Is it good enough for *St. Nicholas*?"

"I think so!"

"Thank you!"

When the next copy of *St. Nicholas* came, Rachel grabbed it, opened it in a hurry, and turned to The St. Nicholas League. Her story was not there.

"They haven't had time to print your story yet," mama told her.

"How long will it take?"

"Two or three months. Maybe longer."

"And maybe," Rachel said, "they never will print it."

"They must get hundreds of stories, dear."

Long months passed. Summer came and went. School began again. One day Rachel opened the September number of *St. Nicholas*. She turned slowly to her favorite part. She jumped up, shouting, "I did it! I did it!" There it was in print, with her name: Rachel L. Carson, age ten.

And there was a letter for Rachel with a check for ten dollars. She made up her mind. "When I grow up, I'll be a writer!"

Chapter 3

"Cash Money"

Now Rachel began to think about the stories mama read them in the evenings—especially the stories about the sea. How could anybody ever learn to write like that?

She had started to high school when she asked, "Mama, how can I learn to be a real writer?"

"First, read all the good books you can. Next, practice writing."

"I do that now!" Rachel said.

"Then, get a good education."

"High school, and then college?"

"Maybe some education after four years of college."

"What else is there?" Rachel asked.

"College people have special names for how much education you have. When you are through college, you have a bachelor's degree. Then you may take special work and get a master's degree. You may even take more work and get a doctor's degree."

"I don't want to be a doctor!"

"It doesn't have anything to do with medicine. It just means you are very, very educated. You are called a Doctor of Philosophy."

"I just want to be a writer."

"Then the first thing is to make good grades in high school. So you'll have a chance to go to college."

"Why?"

"Because we have more land than

'cash money.' Papa keeps hoping to sell some land for building lots, for people to put houses on. But right now people aren't buying. So—well—it takes a lot of money to go to college."

"How much?"

"I'd like to see you go to a college in Pittsburgh—Pennsylvania College for Women. It costs about $1,000 a year. Sometimes colleges give scholarships to bright students who need help. That means the college pays part of the bills for a student with a good record."

"So that's why I'll need good grades —to get a scholarship."

"Yes, dear. Unless times get better, you'll need a scholarship to go to college."

All through high school Rachel worked hard at every subject, whether she liked it or not. By her senior

year, she had a long record of high grades.

"We're proud of you!" mama said.

"It's easy to make top grades in English," Rachel said. "But, oh, that science! I've had enough science to last me the rest of my life!"

"You'll find college more interesting. You'll settle down and take extra work in what you like best. In college they call that your major."

"I know what my major will be!" She wished she could be in college right now. Another half year of high school, then summer vacation. More than six months before she could go to college—if she got a scholarship.

Her English teacher came to see mama. "You want Rachel to go to Pennsylvania College for Women, don't you, Mrs. Carson?"

"Yes," mama said. "We've written to them, but we haven't heard yet."

"I've written to Miss Cora Coolidge, the president of the college," the teacher said. "I've told her about Rachel. Not only top grades, but she has a real gift for writing."

Mama smiled. "Thank you! I'm sure that will help!"

When the teacher had gone, Rachel hugged mama. "I'll get it! I know I'll get it! I wonder how much it will be? Maybe $500? Or maybe the whole $1,000?"

"We'll just have to wait and see."

At last a letter came from the college. Rachel's fingers shook as she opened it.

The college was glad to accept Rachel L. Carson as a student. They were awarding her a $100 scholarship.

Chapter 4

"What's Come Over You?"

Only $100! How could she ever get the other $900 she would need for even one year of college?

"If I can just get started," Rachel said, "I'll work so hard that—that—well, something will *have* to happen!"

Papa scraped together all he could. He'd send her more later, he said, even if he had to borrow it.

When Rachel got to the college, she asked to talk to Miss Coolidge. She told her how things were.

"As mama put it once, 'We have

more land than cash money.' Is there any work I can do to help pay my way through college?"

Miss Coolidge shook her head. "I'm sorry, Rachel. The only thing I can suggest is—do your best and hope for the best."

"I certainly will!" Rachel said.

She often spent her weekends in the library, reading. She spent many long evenings studying and writing.

She took part in everything that had anything to do with writing. She worked on the college newspaper. She sent stories to the college literary magazine. Month after month, her stories were turned down. Finally, at the very end of the year, one of her stories was printed.

Some of the girls said they enjoyed it. "You lucky girl!" one said. "You can just dash off something I'd have to work a month to write!"

Just dash off something! Rachel smiled to herself. If they only knew how many times she wrote even one sentence over and over again! But she was learning! Next year she would keep on learning. By the end of next year . . .

Then she found out a sad fact.

Before she could graduate, she had to have some work in science. What a waste of time! Silly work in a laboratory, looking at bugs through a microscope. Just a lot of crazy words to learn—words that she could never use in a story!

Well, she might as well do it, and get it over with. She'd take biology. All the science majors said Miss Mary Skinker was a wonderful teacher. "She works you like a dog," one said cheerfully, "but what a teacher!"

In September Rachel sighed and walked into her first biology class.

Mary Skinker greeted her with a warm smile. "I read your story last spring, Rachel! I'm so glad to have you in my class!"

"I'm glad one of us is glad," Rachel thought.

But after the class Rachel walked down the hall in a daze. What a teacher! Miss Skinker really did make biology interesting.

Biology—the study of life—everything that lived. One part—botany—was about all the trees and plants and flowers. The other part—zoology—was about all the animals and birds and fish. Biology was about everything!

After a month Rachel began to feel

like two people. One Rachel was making top grades in English and having stories in the college magazine. The other Rachel was thinking about biology—all of life.

Once she got to thinking about biology in English class.

"Rachel Carson," she said to herself, "what's come over you?"

The middle of Rachel's third year, her teachers said it too: "Rachel Carson, what's come over you?" Rachel had changed her major to science.

Even Miss Coolidge sent for her. "Rachel, my dear girl, do you realize what you'll be going through your last year?"

"Yes, Miss Coolidge. At least six classes in science."

"But your wonderful gift for writing, Rachel! You do have that. We have expected you to graduate *magna cum laude*."

Rachel knew what that meant: Cum laude was "with honor." Magna cum laude was "with great honor."

"We have hoped we could get you a full scholarship to work on your master's degree. Please, won't you think about it?"

"I have thought about it, Miss Coolidge. I know I want to work in science the rest of my life. In biology."

Miss Coolidge just shook her head sadly. She didn't argue any longer.

Only Miss Skinker was pleased. "I'll miss you next year, Rachel," she said, "but I know I'll be proud of you!"

"You'll miss me?" Rachel asked.

Miss Skinker was going to Johns Hopkins University to work on her doctor's degree.

Chapter 5

Two Jobs at a Time

Her last year Rachel began work in six classes in science. All the girls but the science majors were fussing at her. Why had she thrown away her chance to be a great writer? What chance was there for her in science?

Rachel did not bother to argue. She did not have time to argue. She was working harder than she had ever worked before. In October she had a letter from Miss Skinker.

"As the girls used to say, 'They are working me like a dog,' but it's a wonderful school. I hope you can come here someday."

Not much chance of that, Rachel knew. She would be in debt when she finished college. Nothing but a full scholarship would help her go to a university to get her master's degree.

Another letter came from Miss Skinker. She was sick. She had had to give up her work at Johns Hopkins. But she still hoped Rachel could go there someday.

In the spring Miss Coolidge sent for Rachel. What was wrong? Rachel could remember that talk last year, when she changed her major to science. She could still see Miss Coolidge shaking her head.

Miss Coolidge was shaking her head again, but she was smiling. "Rachel, you amazing girl!"

Rachel was graduating magna cum laude—"with great honor." She had won a full scholarship to work on her master's degree at Johns Hopkins. And that was not all! In August she would go to Woods Hole, on Cape Cod, Massachusetts.

"You will meet great scientists from all over America," Miss Coolidge said. "Woods Hole is the home of the Marine Biological Laboratory—where men study the life of the sea."

Rachel blinked back tears. She could not keep her voice from shaking. "Oh, Miss Coolidge! I've always dreamed about the ocean. But I've never seen it."

"You certainly will this summer, my dear. At Woods Hole the sea will be all around you."

One morning in August she stood on the deck of a boat, speeding toward

Woods Hole through choppy waters. Again she blinked back tears, though she was smiling. The ocean! How long she had dreamed of it! Now she was on it! She could see it and smell it and feel it as it beat against the boat!

For the six happiest weeks of her life, she studied at Woods Hole. She met men of the U.S. Bureau of Fisheries. She went out with them in a boat as they studied the ocean.

"This is what I want to do someday," she said. "I want to work in the Bureau of Fisheries."

The men smiled. "We don't have women scientists in the Bureau."

"Maybe someday you will!" she said.

They shrugged. She might talk to Elmer Higgins in Washington about it. He was one of the men in charge.

"I'll do that very thing!" she said.

Before her classes started at Johns Hopkins, she went to see Mr. Higgins. She told him what she wanted to do. He was a friendly man. He said there weren't any women scientists in the Bureau. But he wished her luck at Johns Hopkins.

Miss Skinker had been right. They did "work you like a dog" at Johns Hopkins. But Rachel's letters home were cheerful. She didn't say anything about the long, hard days. She didn't say anything about "no place for women scientists."

Mama's letters were cheerful too. She and papa were alone now. Marian was married, and Robert was working in Pittsburgh. They missed Rachel, but they were very proud of her.

Late in October the stock market crashed. Hundreds of men lost all the money they had. Banks failed. Factories closed. Thousands of men were out of work. The Great Depression had begun. Rachel knew that hard times had hit Springdale too.

She found a house that she could rent very cheaply. It was out from Baltimore, but she could take a bus to Johns Hopkins. She wrote mama about it. They would have lean times anywhere. They might as well be together!

Papa found work sometimes in Baltimore. It didn't pay much, but it helped. Rachel got part-time work too. Some of her jobs meant long bus trips back and forth. Sometimes, she thought, she spent half her life going and coming.

All through her work at Johns Hopkins, Rachel did two jobs at a time. After three years she had her master's degree in marine zoology—the life of the sea.

But the Great Depression was still going on. Rachel could not find a place for a woman scientist. There were only part-time jobs and long bus trips.

The summer of 1935 papa died suddenly.

At first Rachel could think of only one thing—how she would miss him. Then words seemed to hammer in her head: *You've got to earn more money!*

Chapter 6

"Fish Tales"

Once more Rachel went to see Elmer Higgins in Washington. He listened; he rubbed his chin. Then he surprised her. "Can you write?"

Rachel had to laugh. "You should have heard the fuss when I changed my major to science!" She told him about college.

"A scientist who can write. I may have a job for you for a few months."

The Bureau of Fisheries was doing short stories for a radio program. "It's called 'Romance under the Waters,'" he said.

"What a lovely name!" Rachel said.

"We just call them the 'Seven Minute Fish Tales,'" he said dryly.

Mr. Higgins had a problem. Several people had tried to do the stories. The writers were not scientists. The men who were scientists could not write.

He gave her samples of the Fish Tales they had done. He gave her subjects for three more. "Take these home and see what you can do. If you can write them, you'll have a job—for a while. It pays about $20 a week—as long as it lasts."

Rachel smiled all the way home. That night right after supper she started on the Fish Tales. At last she stopped, looked up, and listened. Almost dawn! The birds were waking up!

Smiling, she went out and leaned against a tree.

"Hello, birds," she called softly.

Presently all the birds were singing.

"Just like they are talking back to me," she thought. She smiled at the memory.

When Mr. Higgins read her Fish Tales, he nodded. "You have the job. You may work at home or here in our library."

Sometimes Rachel worked at home. Often she worked until the birds woke up. Sometimes she made the long trip to Washington and worked all day in the library.

One evening when she got home, she stopped outside the door, listening. Who was typing so fast? Mama could type, but not that fast. She opened the door quietly and went in. "Mama!"

Mama laughed. "Oh, fiddlesticks! I wanted to surprise you when I got really good."

"You're really good now! You are amazing!"

"What's amazing about it? I know— 'You can't teach an old dog new tricks' —but I'm not 70 yet."

Soon mama was making all the final copies of the Fish Tales. "This is such fun!" she said. "I hope it lasts a long time!"

But Rachel knew it would not.

She heard there was to be an examination for junior aquatic biologist. Marine biologists knew the life of the sea; aquatic biologists would have to know the life of both the sea and the rivers.

She thought back over the years. "If anyone has worked harder or learned more," she told herself, "I'll eat my hat!"

"I hear you want to take the examination?" Mr. Higgins said. "You'll probably be one in a thousand—the only woman."

"I know, Mr. Higgins."

When Rachel went to take the examination, she was the only woman.

The man in charge said, "Yes, young lady? You have something for me?"

"I'm here to take the—"

"What! I thought you were a clerk, with a message for me."

"No, I'm a scientist." Rachel smiled. "A woman scientist."

That evening mama was eager to hear all about it. How soon would Rachel get the job?

Rachel had to laugh. "You're sure I'll make the highest grade?"

"Of course," mama said. "How long before you'll hear about it?"

"Goodness knows." She went back to work on the Fish Tales.

One day she went to the library in Washington.

A clerk said, "Oh, Miss Carson! Don't bother to sit down. Mr. Higgins wants to see you right away."

Rachel's heart sank. Was it the end of the Fish Tales? Was she out of work again?

Chapter 7

Mr. Higgins Says No!

Mr. Higgins came to meet her and held out his hand. "Congratulations! You are now a junior aquatic biologist. And I've asked to have you work for me. How's that?"

"Wonderful!"

"For a while you'll have two jobs."

"I've done that before."

"And you'll be here in the office most of the time."

More long bus trips. But Rachel only smiled. She was a woman scientist!

Her regular job, he said, would be to answer special questions people asked.

"Some questions can be answered with a booklet. Others can't. Those questions will be your job. If you know the answer, good. If you don't, you'll hunt till you find it."

"Yes, sir, Mr. Higgins!"

"And we're going to bring out a book of the Fish Tales. I want you to write an introduction for it."

That Friday evening Rachel wrote her introduction to "Romance under the Waters." Again she was writing when the birds woke up.

Mama read the introduction and looked up with shining eyes. "Why, it's beautiful! To think of writing something beautiful about fish!"

"About the sea," Rachel said. "I think Mr. Higgins will like it."

But Mr. Higgins said, "No, Miss Carson. This isn't any introduction to our Fish Tales. It's a very fine article. Write another introduction for me. Send this to a magazine. You might try *The Atlantic Monthly*."

A fine chance to have something in *The Atlantic Monthly!* Rachel put away her article and wrote another introduction to the Fish Tales.

Then she settled down to answering the questions in letters. Sometimes the days seemed very long.

When she got home, she always stopped outside the door, put on a smile, and then opened the door and called cheerily, "Anybody home?"

One evening mama did not answer. What had happened? "Mama!"

Mama was sitting in a chair, white as a ghost. "Marian is dead."

"Oh, no!" Then Rachel thought of Marian's little girls—just in grade school.

Mama said, "Marjie and Ginny . . ."

"Yes, they'll need a home."

Rachel found a house in Silver Spring, near Washington. She could be home more. She would not have to travel so far.

She sent for the girls. Would she know them? She had not seen them since they were little. Children changed so fast.

She knew them as soon as she saw them. Marjie looked so much like Marian.

"Rachel!" they shouted and came running.

Then her arms were full of two sobbing little girls. She didn't try to talk. By the time they left the station, they had dried their tears and were staring, big-eyed, at the sights.

The house in Silver Spring was a happy one. Mama sang as she baked cookies and smiled when she helped with lessons.

A home took money to run, though. And Rachel knew she had to earn more. She started writing articles for the Sunday section of the Baltimore *Sun*. They didn't earn much. But even fifteen dollars helped.

She wished she had time to write the kind of things she'd like to do. But she could not write all night and sleep in the morning. When she had written the first introduction to the Fish Tales, she had worked till the birds woke up.

She read it over again. Yes, it was good. She made a few changes, and had mama make a fresh copy. She sent it to *The Atlantic Monthly.*

In six weeks a letter brought a check for $75. "Undersea" would be published in September 1937.

She didn't tell Mr. Higgins about it. She waited till she had the magazine. She opened it to "Undersea" and put it on his desk. Wouldn't he be surprised?

But in a few minutes it was Rachel who was surprised. *"What did you say?"*

"I said," Mr. Higgins told her, "that you ought to write a book."

Chapter 8

Three Jobs at a Time

"Write a book!" Rachel gasped. "When would I write it?"

"You've got the heart of a book right here. Every paragraph in this article can be expanded into a chapter. And you'll have a book. Just like that."

Just like that! Did everybody think a writer just dashed off things?

"No, thank you, Mr. Higgins!" She had had enough of two jobs at a time.

But two letters came that changed her mind!

Quincy Howe, editor of Simon and Schuster, wrote. Was Miss Carson writing a book on "Undersea"? His company would like to see it. Hendrik Willem van Loon wrote. *Mr. van Loon! One of the greatest writers in the world!* Surely Miss Carson was doing a book? Mr. van Loon asked.

Rachel knew she was going to do it. But how? And when? How long would it take? A year? Two years? Two years of two jobs at a time?

There were weeks in the next years when she did three jobs at a time: her government work, work on the book, and articles for the *Sun.*

A dozen times in 1939 she thought of giving up. She was so tired. Why did she keep on?

"Just stubbornness!" she told herself. But she knew it was more than that.

She was writing about what she loved, so other people could love it too.

Before the end of 1939, another war was raging overseas. World War II had begun. Rachel remembered when America had entered World War I. Then the ocean had not been a wonderful place to dream about. It was where submarines sneaked around and blew up ships. She used to have nightmares about the ocean.

If she ever dreamed anything now, she did not remember. She just worked and wrote, and fell asleep—if she was not too tired to sleep.

Early in 1941 mama typed the last pages, and Rachel mailed *Under the Sea Wind* to Simon and Schuster.

"How will you celebrate?" Marjie asked.

"If I had time, I'd sleep a week," Rachel told her.

In November 1941 *Under the Sea Wind* was published. The first reviews thrilled mama. *The New York Times* said: "It promises its readers knowledge and sound enjoyment." The *Herald-Tribune* said: "There is drama in every sentence. She rouses our interest in the ocean world and we want to watch it."

Mama smiled. "It makes it worth all the work, doesn't it?"

"Almost . . . "

Then the great Dr. William Beebe wrote, praising the book. He wanted to include two chapters in *The Book of Naturalists*.

Rachel took a deep breath. Yes, maybe it had been worth it. But it would be a long, long time before she'd work that way again!

On December 7, 1941, the Japanese attacked Pearl Harbor. World War II had come to America. War news wiped everything else from people's minds.

The book that had taken three years to write was forgotten in three months.

"Never again!" Rachel said.

All through the war new discoveries about the ocean came to Rachel's desk. Sometimes as she read, she would feel a tingle go up her spine. Nothing in the world was so mysterious as the ocean! If only she had more time . . . No! Not another book!

She was busier than ever with her work. The Bureau of Fisheries became the Fish and Wildlife Service. Now she studied the migrations of the birds. She visited many of the wildlife refuges.

By 1948 she was editor-in-chief of books of the Fish and Wildlife Service. She had an office of her own, with five people working under her.

Even men! She had to smile at that.

By 1948 the war-time secrets of the ocean could be published. Rachel read everything she could find. At last she sighed and shook her head.

"Here I go again!" She was going to write another book!

She decided she'd get a literary agent to help her.

A young friend in Washington recommended Mrs. Marie Rodell.

"Of course, she is a woman," he said, "but she's got a fine reputation."

"A woman scientist shouldn't object to a woman literary agent," Rachel said.

She soon found out how much help a good agent could be.

In 1949, long before the book was done, Marie Rodell had a contract with Oxford University Press. But—Oxford wanted the manuscript in ten months!

Chapter 9

Time Enough

"I can't possibly finish it in ten months!" Rachel said.

"Why not get a leave of absence from your job? Take time off?"

"I can't afford to."

Marie Rodell smiled. "You've heard of foundations, haven't you?"

"Guggenheim, Ford—that sort of thing? Yes. I know they make grants to colleges."

"The best thing they do with their

money is to make grants to writers who are working on really important books."

Rachel wrote to Dr. Beebe about it. "A sound idea!" Dr. Beebe said. He and Edwin Way Teale, the famous naturalist, both knew and admired her work. They would be glad to put in a good word for her. Soon she had a grant from the Saxton Memorial Fund.

She had enough money to take time off, but it was not so easy to walk out of her office. She took a month off—then found double work piled up and waiting for her when she got back. Oxford had wanted the book by February. It was July of 1950 before *The Sea Around Us* went to them.

Not long after that, Marie Rodell had sent her a special message. Houghton Mifflin wanted Rachel to write a guidebook about the life of the seashore.

"Oh, no!" Rachel said.

"We'll get a grant that's big enough for you to take a whole year off."

A whole year just to write? Rachel signed the contract.

"But I don't have a deadline," Rachel told mama. "They'll get the book when it is done. Now I can rest in peace. Oxford and Marie Rodell are taking care of *The Sea Around Us*."

"What else is there for Mrs. Rodell to do?" mama asked.

"She wants to sell parts of the book to magazines to be published before the book comes out."

"Won't that hurt the sale of the book?"

"She says it will help. And I think she knows her business."

A chapter of the book came out in *Yale Review*. It won a $1,000 prize for the best magazine science writing of the year.

Then *The New Yorker* wanted to do three parts of the book. Of all things! It was a smart "citified" magazine. It printed "Profiles"—stories about famous people. Now it would do "Profile of the Sea"! And the price made mama gasp.

The *Reader's Digest* offered $10,000 to do the book in a short form for their condensed books.

Meantime, Dr. Beebe and Mr. Teale were "going to bat" for Rachel. A grant of $4,000 came from the Guggenheim Foundation. In June of 1951 Rachel began her leave of absence for a year. A whole year to do nothing but study the seashore and get ready to write the next book!

Rachel celebrated by going to a beach she loved. A whole year of enough time and peace!

In July *The Sea Around Us* was published. That was the end of lazy days at the seashore.

The Sea Around Us was on the best seller list of the *Times*, and was a Book-of-the-Month Club selection. By Christmas time it was selling 4,000 copies a day.

Marie Rodell persuaded Oxford to publish *Under the Sea Wind* again. The book that had been forgotten in 1941 was on the best seller list in 1952. Two books by one author were on a best seller list at the same time!

Rachel gave back the Guggenheim grant. She resigned from her job. Now she had money and time to write anything she wanted to write!

But she found it took a lot of time to be famous. There were phone calls and letters. There were speeches to make and books to autograph. She had to be honored at receptions, luncheons, and dinners.

"I have money enough," she thought, "and I'll have time enough as soon as I get done being famous!"

When Marie Rodell read the first chapters of *The Edge of the Sea*, she said, "You're going to have another best seller."

"Please, not that!" Rachel said. "I have another book I want to write!"

Chapter 10

"It's Up to You!"

In 1955 *The Edge of the Sea* was published. Marie Rodell had been right: a Profile in *The New Yorker*, weeks on the best seller list, Book-of-the-Month Club, and *Reader's Digest* condensed books.

Rachel was glad when summer came and she could go to Maine. It was her favorite place in the whole world.

Marjie and Ginny were both married now. Marjie was a widow with a little son. From the time Roger was two, he

trotted along with Rachel to the woods and the beach.

Early in 1957, when Roger was five, Marjie died.

Mama said, "What will become of Roger?"

"I'll adopt him," Rachel said. "I am closer to him than anybody else."

"I'll help all I can," mama promised.

Mama was very crippled with arthritis now, but she could still read poems and stories as she had when Rachel was a little "tagalong."

Rachel was deep in plans for the next book, but Roger was never lonesome.

Now and then Marie Rodell reported that some magazine had offered a huge fee for an article.

"Tell them NO! The book I'm working on will take five years; the next one I want to write will take another five! And nobody, but nobody, is going to change my mind!"

Early in 1958 she got a letter with a newspaper clipping from Mrs. Olga Owens Huckins, a long-time friend. Planes had sprayed their region with DDT to kill mosquitoes. She had written to a paper:

> The "harmless" shower bath killed seven of our lovely song birds outright. . . . The next day three more were scattered around the bird bath. (I had emptied it and scrubbed it after the spraying BUT YOU CAN NEVER KILL DDT.)

Please, Mrs. Huckins wrote, would Rachel find someone who could stop this dreadful killing?

Rachel tried. She wrote a dozen letters. Then one answer jolted her:

"Rachel Carson, you are the one person in the world to do this! A scientist who can write! *It's up to you!*"

"I'll write a brief book," she said.

She began to collect the facts. The grim reports poured in. A cold chill crawled through Rachel.

Those "wonderful, magical" pesticides were the deadliest thing man had ever spread on the earth. More reports . . . Soon Rachel was sending out hundreds of letters all over the world.

She knew now it could not be a brief book. It was going to take more time to collect all the facts than any book she had ever done.

Those facts had to be right! She knew she was going to have a fight on her hands. Pesticides were "big business." Big chemical companies were making millions of dollars out of them.

"I'll help all I can," mama said. But in December, she died.

For weeks Rachel was numb with sorrow. How could she go on? But she had to go on! She could not forget those words: *"It's up to you!"*

Her days had three parts now: "Readin', Ritin', and Roger." Even though she had a good housekeeper, Roger needed her time. How often he ran in, calling, "Rachel! Look what I found!"

And why was she getting so tired? Why did she feel so draggy?

During the spring of 1960, she went to Washington to see her doctor. "Find out why I am so tired, and put me back in shape. I have work to do!"

Doctors operated. It was a tumor, they said, but not a cancer. She ought to be feeling fit very soon again.

But she did not feel fit soon again. Even with a fine secretary, she could never get enough done.

She sent a sample chapter of the book to a long-time friend who was a scientist.

"You're doing a magnificent job," he told her. "But I doubt it will be a best seller. You'd better be ready for quite a battle."

"I won't care if I do have a fight on my hands," she told him. "The more they rave, the more people will read. *I'll do this book if it's the last thing I ever do!*"

Late in 1960 she found out it would be just that—the last book she would live to write.

Chapter 11

The Last Book

The doctors finally told her the truth. She did have cancer. They could not get it all when they had operated. Now it was spreading. Yes, they said, they could give treatments.

"Just so I can keep on working," she said. "And one thing . . . "

"Yes, Miss Carson?"

"I'm going to say I have arthritis. People don't dither at you so if you say you have arthritis. I will not have people dithering over me!"

Day after day, week after week, the work on the book went on. Fact after fact proved what man was doing to his world: poisoning the air, the earth, the water; killing birds, the fish, and man himself.

The name of the book, *Silent Spring,* came from a poem by Keats:

> The sedge is wither'd from the lake
> And no birds sing.

Rachel finished the book early in 1962. It would be published in September. But *Silent Spring* made headlines long before September. The Profile started in *The New Yorker* in June.

It shocked the nation. For the first time most people knew of the danger of DDT and other pesticides.

Letters poured in to Rachel, to the magazine, to Washington.

The chemical companies fought back. They spent thousands to try to prove that *Silent Spring* was just a silly thing by "that hysterical woman, Rachel Carson." As one newspaper said it, *"Silent Spring* became a noisy summer!"

CBS asked Rachel if she would be willing to face her accusers on a television show.

"Nothing could please me more!" Rachel said.

CBS announced that "The *Silent Spring* of Rachel Carson" would be seen on April 3, 1963. For months before the date CBS worked to do the show and put it on tape.

An odd thing happened. Letters poured in to CBS about a show that had not been seen. *"Don't do that show!"* But CBS did do the show.

Rachel watched it at home in Silver Spring and was glad. The book had been on the best seller list. Thousands of people had read it. But millions of people had seen the television show.

That summer she went to Maine for the last time. She knew it would be the last time. Roger, a sturdy little eleven-year-old, raced and shouted and found things and brought them to show to Rachel. It was a good summer. If only it could last longer.

She lay with binoculars and watched the flights of the birds to the south. She stayed until autumn made the trees a blaze of color. She watched one last moonrise over the water. Then she said good-bye to Maine and went back to Silver Spring.

One night in April she told her nurse, "I want you to waken me at 5:30 tomorrow morning."

"But, Miss Carson, it won't be light yet."

"I know. And I want you to wheel me out in the yard under the trees."

"Yes, Miss Carson."

In the morning a hand shook her gently. "Miss Carson, you said to waken you."

"Yes! It's very special!"

Rachel held the flashlight as the nurse wheeled her out into the yard. "This is fine. Thank you. I have the bell. I'll ring when I want you."

"Yes, Miss Carson."

Rachel switched off the flashlight and sat in the dark. At last she heard a sleepy little twitter, then another, and presently all the birds were singing.

"Good-bye, birds," she called softly. "I'll not be around long. But I hope you'll be here for a long, long time!"

She died on April 14, 1964. A service was held in Washington Cathedral. Senators, congressmen, and government officials were there to honor her. And many, many people who knew her only through her books.

Legend has it that Lincoln once said to Harriet Beecher Stowe, "So you are the little lady who started this big war."

Rachel Carson was the little lady who started another war—the fight against the careless use of deadly chemicals.